RELAX TO RICHES WORKBOOK

RENEE ROSE

RENEE ROSE ROMANCE

Copyright © December 2024 Relax to Riches Workbook by Renee Rose and Renee Rose Romance

All rights reserved. This copy is intended for the original purchaser of this book ONLY. No part of this book may be reproduced, scanned, or distributed in any printed or electronic form without prior written permission from the authors. Please do not participate in or encourage piracy of copyrighted materials in violation of the authors' rights. Purchase only authorized editions.

Published in the United States of America

Wilrose Dream Ventures LLC

Cover image by Regina Wamba

Cover Design by Kasmit Covers

❀ Created with Vellum

Hello Beautiful!

This workbook is dedicated to you—wonderful, magical you.
I'm so honored you read Relax to Riches and want to take it a step further by digging into the workbook.

Honoring yourself this way will allow you to connect with your deepest source of wisdom, power and authenticity. Abundance can only be the natural result!

Get your sleep spa ready, find the perfect pen, and dive in to receive so much more from yourself and your life!

XXOO
Renee

ABOUT THIS WORKBOOK

I'm so glad you're joining me on this journey.

This workbook is to be used in conjunction with the *Relax to Riches* book, and will take you through the process of integration step-by-step.

With the use of these tools, you will know yourself as a being of light. As a powerful manifester. You will love yourself as you are right now, shadow and all. You will have the basis, the steady platform from which to launch and grow any creation. To meet the love of your life. Have your dream job. To move into your dream house. To drive your dream car. But most importantly, you will know that it's not any of those things that truly make you rich. Rather, it is your belief in yourself. It is a sense of wholeness, wellness, and integration.

It is breaking up with the habit of rejecting parts of yourself and wishing you were someone else, or were in a different place, or had a different life.

When you have your own back, there's nothing you lack and

ABOUT THIS WORKBOOK

nothing that can be taken from you. And that is true abundance.

For resources or more information, enter your email at https://relax2riches.com.

NOTE:

The information presented in the Relax to Riches book and workbook is not intended to diagnose mental health problems or to take the place of the professional mental health care provided by a licensed clinical professional therapist.

This book does not constitute an attempt to practice trauma or clinical therapy. Individuals should consult a licensed clinical mental health care provider for mental health advice and answers to personal mental health questions, especially regarding (but not limited to) traumatic events.

HOW TO USE THE WORKBOOK

*I*n this workbook, we will explore nine energetic tools that will help you relax into your power as a manifester, so you can create everything you desire with total ease:

1. Find the Frequency
2. Unpack Unworthiness
3. Fear is Freedom
4. Sleep to Success
5. Live to Laugh
6. Welcome the Wins
7. Consume Cannibals
8. Purge Pain
9. Give Up Guilt

This workbook follows the above order, but you don't have to fill it in or follow in that order.

You may choose to use your workbook more like a tarot deck—holding it in your hands and setting your intention to open to the prompt or section that has exactly what you need that day, then seeing what page the workbook opens on.

I suggest journaling first thing in the morning when your subconscious is still fresh, but any time you're called to it is perfect.

You don't have to fill all the lines allotted. If you find there isn't enough room to write, feel free to use the additional sheets at the back, add notebook paper, or continue in your own journal.

Freewriting

We will utilize freewriting as a method of accessing your inner knowing. If you haven't played with it as an exercise before, here are the basic tenets:

- Keep your pen moving across the page and shut off the internal editor as you freewrite answers to the prompts.
- Don't think—just write.
- Write the first answer that pops into your mind, or sometimes it will feel you write before you even cognitively know the answer.
- Write until nothing more comes out for each prompt, then move on to the next one.

You're tapping into your subconscious or intuition to get the answers. Don't try to get the right answer or to answer from your cognitive brain—conclusions limit possibilities. Instead, use your perception and awareness and allow them space on the page and in your consciousness.

If you get tired or feel exhausted, take a break and come back to it later. When you truly allow yourself to fully explore, it can be a lot for your nervous system to absorb. You're bringing the anti-consciousness—the knowledge you are resisting in your life—into consciousness. There are things we stick our heads in the sand about—this will uncover them. You're moving to a life in which you truly embody and live in clarity, which will translate to abundance if you choose to receive it. Riches can be your easy norm when you're fully integrated.

PREPARATION

I included many exercises and home play opportunities in this workbook, but not one of them is required. The premise is to relax, and if learning these tools feels like work, we're in the wrong energy.

That said, if you want to go all in, here are some steps you might take to prepare. I suggest you work through one tool per week. If you're looking for a buddy or friend to go through the program with, there is information at the end of the book on how to set up your own study group. I also recommend joining the Relax to Riches Facebook group for a supportive community to share your insights, progress, and questions.

One of the key steps in *Relax to Riches* is Sleep to Success. We will use the fertile time of dreaming to reprogram our subconscious for what we want to manifest. To that end, it's useful to think about your sleep routine and where you sleep and become conscious and intentional about making it a sacred space. While it is not necessary to go out and spend a lot of money to make your sleeping space special, investing in a few incremental upgrades is a powerful message to your subconscious and the Universe that you are willing to honor yourself, your intention, and your alignment with abundance.

Again, this step isn't required to deepen your manifestation practice. If it stops you from going on, if it creates a reason for you to procrastinate going through the steps of this book, then skip it! By all means, you can do the whole ritual the next time you go through this book.

But rituals work with the subconscious. They tell your brain to pay attention, that what you are doing is important. When you take the time to prepare, you will fast-track into your power and potency by signaling to your brain that the journey into consciousness you are about to embark on is significant, relevant, and important.

1. **Set up Your Dream Spa**

Prepare your very own dream spa. We want to create the feeling of being pampered, taking care of yourself, and opening yourself to the Universe. When you do that, the Universe matches your vibe.

You may want to think about making some incremental upgrades to your sleeping space. Pretend you're sleeping at the Four Seasons. Do you have Four Seasons-worthy bedding? What would a luxurious bed be for you?

What does *cozy* mean to you? Our subconscious mind's primary purpose is to keep us alive and safe. The feeling of cozy equates with the sensation of safety, of home, of a feathered nest. When you feel *cozy*, your subconscious mind will feel safe, and it will relax and open to the suggestions you're going to give it.

Here are some ideas of how you might make your sleep space at the least, cozy, and at best, a luxurious and sacred space:

- Fluff up your bed with a nest of different sizes and shapes of pillows
- Buy yourself a new pillowcase and / or duvet. Consider natural fabrics like cotton, linen, silk, bamboo or hemp, as natural fabrics have high vibrations. I have a very soft plush throw blanket I was given as a gift for Christmas that makes my bed a cozy dream sanctuary now.
- Relocate some candles to your bedroom. (Use battery-operated for safety or make blowing them out before you turn off the light a step in your ritual.)
- Clear the clutter to make your sleep space a sanctuary.
- Bring in essential oils that promote relaxation and sleep. My favorites are lavender, Frankincense, and lemon balm. Other good bedtime oils include Jasmine, Chamomile, Sandalwood, Valerian, Vetiver Oil, or Cedarwood. Choosing what is pleasing to you is always the best way to pick!
- Use a salt or selenite lamp or some other form of soothing lighting near your bed
- Try a silk lavender eye pillow with weight to create a spa-like experience.

2. **Create a Sleep-Spa Ritual.**

Make new rules about your bedtime hygiene. Rules are more important to the subconscious than things you relegate to "it would be nice". Just like the act of creating a dream board at the beginning of the year, you are setting a powerful intention to use your dream time to create. The ritual of your routine sinks into the subconscious, programming it for your desired outcome.

Evaluate your current bedtime routine and tweak it until it completely supports sleep and dream-time as sacred, rejuvenating, and nourishing. What routine would make you feel relaxed, pampered, and ready to enter your spa?

True confession—I'm speaking to myself here. There are so many times I stay up until I'm exhausted, and then I skip washing my face or putting on PJs and fast track my way to bed by means of a quick brush of my teeth and removing my bra and pants, climbing under the covers in whatever shirt I wore that day and a pair of undies.

This is *not* the vibe we're going for here.

Instead, set up a bedtime ritual that begins before you're exhausted. Start 20 or 30 minutes earlier than usual to take time with your routine. Come up with steps that are right for you.

Here are some suggestions based on what I love to do to make my dream time delicious. When I do these steps, I find myself excited to go to bed, almost giddy for my delicious spa-like experience where I'm entering the realm of the mystical to pull it into the physical.

- Turn off the TV, put your phone away, and put on relaxing music as you wind down.
- Take a bath before bed, using Epsom salts to relax your muscles or a tablespoon of baking soda to detox. Add in your favorite essential oils like frankincense or lavender. If you prefer showers, bring the Epsom salts into the

shower as a salt rub and spray your favorite oils into the shower mist.
- Wash your face and put on your best skin cream. Take the time for all those indulgences you usually skip, like wearing a facemask or using the fancy exfoliating scrub.
- Put on some comfy pajamas.
- Do some gentle stretches to relax your muscles. You could watch and follow a yoga Nidra video (geared toward restful sleep) on YouTube.
- Use an LED light or lie on an LED mat to melt away your aches and pains. I have a heated one on my bed that I use as I'm falling asleep (links in the Resources section at the end of this book).

3. **Dedicate a Notebook For Your Relax to Riches Journal**

In addition to this workbook, keep a blank journal and pen or pencil beside your bed. You will use it for freewriting exercises, morning pages, to document what you intend to dream about, and the manifestations you are calling into being. You may use it again in the morning to record your dreams.

4. **Download My Lucid Dreaming Meditation**

Download the lucid dreaming meditations from the https://Relax2Riches.com page to use as you're falling asleep. Put it on your phone or wherever you listen to music, so it's easily accessible when you're ready for bed.

TOOL #1

Find the Frequency

HOME PLAY

1. This week, practice your sleep spa ritual each night.
2. Keep this workbook or a blank *Relax to Riches* journal beside your bed and jot down any dreams you have when you wake. If you don't remember your dreams, use the first five minutes of waking to record your intentions for the day or your answers to the magic wand freewriting exercise from this chapter.

FIND THE FREQUENCY OF WHAT YOU DESIRE

Find the frequency of what you desire—your *real* why. **Imagine you have a magic wand,** and you've already waved it with the command to deliver your perfect future. Think about each of the following areas of your life: relationships, finances, job / occupation, social life / activities, home, travel / life experiences, body. Freewrite on what a magic-wanded future might look like in each of these areas.

Relationships

Who is in your life, and what do you do together?

How do you feel in your relationship(s)?

What would you magically change about your present relationship(s)?

_____
_____
_____
_____
_____
_____
_____
_____
_____
_____

Finances

How much money do you have in your bank account?

_____
_____
_____
_____
_____
_____

RENEE ROSE

How much do you earn a month? A year?

What are you doing with your excess of money?

How do you treat yourself?

How does it feel to be rich? What does your day look like?

Job/Occupation

What are you doing each day?

_____
_____
_____
_____
_____
_____
_____
_____

How is your work received by others / the world?

_____
_____
_____
_____
_____
_____
_____
_____

Social life / activities

What do you do for fun?

_____
_____
_____
_____
_____
_____
_____
_____
_____
_____

What new experiences are available to you?

_____
_____
_____
_____
_____
_____
_____
_____

Do you travel? If so, where do you go?

_____
_____
_____
_____
_____
_____
_____
_____
_____
_____

Who do you spend your time with?

_____
_____
_____
_____
_____
_____
_____
_____

What does your leisure time look and feel like?

_____
_____
_____
_____
_____
_____
_____
_____
_____
_____
_____

Home

What does your home look like?

_____
_____
_____
_____
_____
_____
_____
_____

Where do you live?

RENEE ROSE

What's the view from your window?

What luxuries do you surround yourself with?

Do you feel cozy? Expansive? (What's the *feeling* of being in your perfect home?)

Body

How do you feel in your body?

_____
_____
_____
_____
_____
_____
_____
_____
_____
_____
_____
_____
_____
_____
_____
_____
_____
_____
_____
_____
_____
_____
_____
_____

Are you strong and flexible with vibrant health and well-being?

Does your weight feel balanced for you?

How do you look?

How do you feel when you walk into a room with your gorgeous body?

TOOL #2

Unpack Unworthiness

HOME PLAY

1. Continue with your sleep spa ritual each night.
2. Record your dreams each morning or work on the freewriting exercises in this tool.
3. Try the Expanding to Become Multidimensional Meditation. Find the free download at https://Relax2Riches.com
4. Complete the Worthiness Freewriting Exercise and the Shadow Discovery Freewriting Exercise.

WORTHINESS FREEWRITING EXERCISE

Freewrite (write the first answer that pops into your head, or better yet, don't even think, just move your pen across the page) on the following prompts.

Where am I striving or trying to achieve something in my life?

_____
_____
_____
_____
_____
_____
_____
_____

On a scale of 1-10, how worthy do I feel of receiving what I'm asking for *today / right now*?

_____
_____
_____
_____
_____
_____
_____
_____

Where do I think I need to earn it?

How do I think I need to earn it?

Where am I looking for outside measures of my self worth? (e.g., best seller list, number of followers, a number in the bank account, a number of students enrolled in a course)

_____
_____
_____
_____
_____
_____
_____
_____
_____
_____
_____
_____
_____
_____
_____
_____
_____
_____
_____
_____
_____
_____

Am I willing to believe I am worthy right now, before I've achieved those successes? (Affirm it in writing below!)

Where have I deflected gifts from the Universe?

SHADOW DISCOVERY FREEWRITING EXERCISE

What am I unwilling to be that if I embrace it would change everything for me?

_____
_____
_____
_____
_____
_____
_____
_____
_____
_____
_____
_____
_____

How do I define myself?

RENEE ROSE

Where might the opposite or something else actually be true?

What do other people say about me that I resist or align with?

What am I actively rejecting in my self-image or feel shameful about?

How/where can I shine radical acceptance for parts of myself? How do I feel when I do that?

___
___
___
___
___
___
___
___
___
___
___
___
___
___
___
___
___
___
___
___
___
___
___
___
___
___

EXPANDING TO BECOME MULTIDIMENSIONAL MEDITATION

*U*se this visualization or meditation to integrate your divided energies or will.

Imagine a coin

Imagine a coin, which represents our two unintegrated sides—conscious and unconscious—light and shadow.

The heads side is light, and the other side is shadow. The heads side represents the conscious mind and your conscious intention. The dark side represents your shadow side or your subconscious resistance. Your shadow side isn't bad—it encompasses your repressed desires, such as the desire to stay safe, to stay small, not to stretch or grow. Because these are two sides of a coin, there's no getting rid of one of the sides. They both are you. The shadow side can't be "cleared."

Expand the coin to become a sphere

Now, imagine the flat coin expanding like a blowfish and turning into a clear orb, like a snow globe. The coin transforms from a flat two-dimensional object into a three-dimensional sphere. It fills with the energies of both sides of you. Visualize them mingling and getting to know one another. As the energies move together, they swirl. Light blends with smoke. As you continue to watch it transform, colors and patterns may emerge. As with oil and vinegar, they probably won't fully mix, but rather, they learn to interact with one another and form a generative relationship.

The longer you hold this in your awareness, you may see beautiful swirls and patterns, like the opening of a flower or spirals of energy.

Like a snow globe after it's been shaken, the energies are dispersed into the whole or throughout the whole orb. In this way, the shadow side integrates wills with the conscious side, and this creates a power. The shadow side actually helps fuel the rocket of the whole.

TOOL #3

Fear is Freedom

HOME PLAY

1. Continue with your sleep spa ritual
2. Record your dreams in your *Relax to Riches* journal
3. Writing practice: Complete the Deepest Fears Inventory
4. Practice the Dissolve Your Fears in Light Meditation

DEEPEST FEAR INVENTORY

*C*omplete this "Deepest Fear Inventory" developed by Dr. Carolyn Elliot and outlined in her book *Existential Kink*.

Dear Universe (or what resonates for you),
    I   hate   and   resent   [the   thing   you   wish   to   manifest]
_____

because I have deep fear that I....

1. _____
2. _____
3. _____
4. _____
5. _____
6. _____
7. _____
8. _____
9. _____
10. _____

11. _____
12. _____
13. _____
14. _____
15. _____
16. _____
17. _____
18. _____
19. _____
20. _____

Say: *"Dear Universe, I ask that you remove these deepest fears. I pray for knowledge of your will for me and the power to carry it out. Thank you."*

Dr. Elliott recommends you read it to someone else to witness (no feedback, just witnessing, then tear it into tiny pieces.

DISSOLVE YOUR FEARS IN LIGHT MEDITATION

*I*f you'd like to take a step beyond asking the Universe to remove the fears, actually leaning into them—pulling them into your light and thereby fully owning and transmuting them yourself—can be a powerful way to integrate. Follow the steps below, or download a guided meditation from https://Relax2Riches.com.

1. Begin by visualizing your being as a giant ball of light extending three feet beyond your physical body in all directions.
2. Imagine there's a candlewick in the center of your chest behind your sternum. Light the wick there and keep your attention on it as a golden light grows, bathing your heart region in healing light.
3. Grow it even bigger until it fills your entire ball of light.
4. Now imagine you just crumpled the page with all your fears into a tight wad of paper.
5. Bring the crumpled wad into the flame in your heart and keep your attention on it until it has completely burned, until even the ashes have burned, until there's not one speck left of those fears.

6. Return your focus to the light in the center of your chest and notice how those fears fueled your light. Just like putting a log on a fire makes it grow brighter, so did this integration of your fears into your heart center. You now are a stronger, brighter, more integrated person who has dealt with her fears and absorbed them.

TOOL #4

Sleep To Success

HOME PLAY

1. Continue with your sleep spa rituals.
2. Once a week, listen to a subliminal recording as you sleep.
3. Record your dreams in your *Relax to Riches* journal, noting themes.
4. Play with a dreaming exercise—either "Dream it into Being" or lucid dreaming—and record your dreams in your *Relax to Riches* journal.
5. Interpret and heal using any of the methods in this section.
6. Play with lucid dreaming and record your dreams in your *Relax to Riches* journal, looking for themes.
7. Practice one of the healing methods described in this section for healing a dream part.
8. Complete the Dream Theme Freewriting exercise.

PROGRAMMING YOUR SUBCONSCIOUS

P.M. Thought or energy I intend to program into my subconscious while I sleep:

_____
_____
_____
_____
_____
_____

Listen to some kind of "consciousness programming" recording right before you go to bed or as you sleep.

A.M.

My emotional state upon waking:

_____
_____
_____
_____
_____
_____
_____
_____

I dreamed about:

_____
_____
_____
_____
_____
_____
_____
_____
_____
_____
_____
_____

Themes in my dream:

What did the dream mean? (Just write and see what comes out)

RENEE ROSE

What is the most important thing for me to do today?

_____
_____
_____
_____
_____
_____

How can I resolve _____ [dilemma]?

_____
_____
_____
_____
_____
_____
_____
_____
_____
_____
_____
_____

What does Spirit want me to know today?

RENEE ROSE

What message is there for me from Source energy? (or my higher self, or my highest possible guides, or the Universe?)

DREAM IT INTO BEING

.M.

1. Download the "Dream it into Being" sleep induction (https://Relax2Riches.com)
2. I'm going to dream about

   _____
   _____

3. Listen to the "Dream it into Being" recording before you fall asleep and remind yourself throughout the night of what you're asking to dream about.

RENEE ROSE

A.M.

My emotional state upon waking:

_____
_____
_____
_____
_____
_____

I dreamed about:

_____
_____
_____
_____
_____
_____
_____
_____
_____
_____
_____
_____
_____

Themes in my dream:

What did the dream mean? (Just write and see what comes out)

RENEE ROSE

What is the most important thing for me to do today?

How can I resolve _____ [dilemma]?

RENEE ROSE

What does Spirit want me to know today?

What message is there for me from Source energy? (or my higher self, or my highest possible guides, or the Universe?)

LUCID DREAMING

.M.

1. Throughout the day(s), **start to ask yourself if you're dreaming**. This will trigger you to ask yourself at night, and you'll realize you're in a dream.
2. Continue with your sleep wind-down practice, keeping that "sleep-spa" vibe, so your bed is a sacred intuitive space.
3. I intend to lucid dream about

_____

4. Listen to the "Lucid Dreaming Sleep Induction" recording by entering your email at https://relax2riches.com or one of the ones on *Insight Timer* like those included in the Resources section of *Relax to Riches*.
5. As you dream, try to notice if any of your common dream themes come up. Just like you reminded yourself what you wanted to dream about over the past nine days, now you'll intend to become lucid.
6. If you become lucid, actively mold the images to your pleasure. You can create anything. It doesn't have to be

real. In fact, make it fantastical and outlandish. Picture yourself rolling in heaps of money. Leap like a gazelle, do a backflip, race a cheetah. Imagine standing before a stadium of people, and they're all chanting your name. Play with images that give you the frequency of what you're going for–of abundance, of success, of empowerment. This is the way you create a future you can live in.

7. Record any dreams / experiences you had or insights in your *Relax to Riches* journal. Feel free to share any experiences in my Relax to Riches Facebook group.

A.M.

My emotional state upon waking:

_____
_____
_____
_____
_____
_____
_____

I dreamed about:

_____
_____
_____
_____
_____
_____
_____
_____
_____
_____
_____
_____
_____

Themes in my dream:

What did the dream mean? (Just write and see what comes out)

RENEE ROSE

What is the most important thing for me to do today?

_____
_____
_____
_____
_____
_____

How can I resolve ____ [dilemma]?

_____
_____
_____
_____
_____
_____
_____
_____
_____
_____

RENEE ROSE

What does Spirit want me to know today?

What message is there for me from Source energy? (or my higher self, or my highest possible guides, or the Universe?)

DREAM ANALYSIS

*L*ist common themes or emotions you've noticed in your dreams.

_____
_____
_____
_____
_____
_____
_____
_____
_____
_____
_____
_____
_____

Where else in my life am I feeling this way?

When is the first time I remember feeling this way? How old was I? What was happening?

List common people / figures in your dreams.

_____
_____
_____
_____
_____
_____
_____
_____

List the location / environment in your dreams.

_____
_____
_____
_____
_____
_____
_____
_____

HEALING A DREAM FIGURE

1. Call them to the white floor in the space of nothingness or to the top of the crystal mountain to talk.
2. Recognize that they are a part of yourself.
3. If it's not clear, ask, *what are you trying to show me?*
4. If you don't get an answer from that question, know that it will come to you. Simply asking the question opens the door for the answer to come in.
5. Tell them you received the lesson.
6. Acknowledge the gifts they are presenting you with.
7. Thank them for what they're showing you in your dreams.

WORKING WITH A FRACTURED PART OF YOU

1. Call the character (or setting) in your dream (or fractured self) up in your mind. Where do you feel they reside in your body? For example, do you feel a tightness in your chest when you think about them?
2. Ask them to meet you on the white floor in the room of nothingness.
3. Face them and see them as one of your teammates. They are not an adversary to try to clear or work against. They are showing up to help you, to gift you what they believe you need to stay safe and survive.
4. Ask what gifts they're trying to give you. How are they trying to keep you safe or protect you in some way?
5. Thank them for those gifts.
6. If the gift is unwanted (like in my case, making me invisible), tell them you no longer require this form of protection. You appreciate their help, but you can take it from here.
7. Ask them if they can find a new way to stand at your side and support you.

8. When you have a sense that they've agreed, imagine that character stepping into your body and dissolving into the power of you. You absorb them and become more powerful as a result of it. Notice if the initial feeling in your body has changed.

WORKING WITH YOUNGER SELF

1. Ask the question, *what age was I when I first experienced this?* See if a certain event comes to mind. If you don't have a specific, you can make one up. For example, the bloody nose incident of middle school stands out for me, but it really represents those entire three years of friendlessness and feeling like an outcast.
2. Call that memory self onto the white floor in the room of nothingness.
3. Face them and be sure you are viewing them with compassion.
4. If you're having trouble seeing them with compassion, change them into a different avatar.
5. Rewatch the memory or imagined scene with the eyes of compassion. Have sympathy for what that younger self went through. Note that they weren't to blame for whatever it was that happened. They were doing the very best they could in the situation they were in.
6. Now show your memory self that the decisions they made in that moment are no longer (or actually never were) true. That you are successful, loved, and highly

capable. You no longer require the self-image they adopted that says anything otherwise.
7. Let your memory self know that she's safe. She never has to return to that time. She can come with you to the present. Ask her what she needs from you.
8. Scoop your memory self up and give her a cuddle (if that's what she would like). Maybe she just wants to be witnessed, listened to, and validated. After you give her what she needs, let the memory dissolve into sparkles. What color are the sparkles? Alternatively, you could put the scene into a burning flame to incinerate it. What color was the flame? What scent would you pick to go with this scene?
9. If you could pick a wild animal or mythical creature that represented the new, integrated you, what would it be?
10. Use the scent and spirit guide animal as anchors if you feel the feeling again. Call up the spirit animal and the scent and remind yourself that you've updated and integrated your system.

DREAM THEME FREEWRITING EXERCISE

Freewrite on the following prompts. Be sure to turn off your conscious mind / editor. Let these answers come from your gut—the first thing that comes out. Follow the creative thread to see what emerges.

Once you've looked at the themes and deeper meaning to your dreams, determine if there's a part of you asking to be listened to, heard, and healed. Follow the suggested steps for working with and healing a memory-self or an unclaimed or fractured part of yourself.

What does the theme [pick one theme to explore] in my dreams mean to me?

_____
_____
_____
_____
_____
_____
_____
_____
_____
_____
_____
_____
_____
_____
_____
_____
_____
_____
_____
_____
_____
_____
_____
_____
_____
_____

In what way is [pick a person from your dream] an aspect of myself?

What does the setting [pick a particular setting] represent to me?

USING YOUR SLEEP SPA FOR INTUITIVE ANSWERS

P.M. Tonight I intend to dream about [question you desire the answer to or a person you want to dream]

_____
_____
_____
_____
_____
_____
_____
_____
_____
_____
_____
_____

A.M.
What I remember from my dreams:

USING YOUR SLEEP SPA FOR HEALING

P.M.
Tonight, I intend to heal:

_____
_____
_____
_____
_____
_____

Consciously connect with the area of your body that requires healing. If you're in pain, try finding the center point of it and go in to loosen its grip on you.

Body, what are you trying to tell me with this issue?

RENEE ROSE

Body, what do you require? (write whatever comes out)

Place your hands on your body in the place where you're experiencing the pain or simply on your chest or belly. Intend that the frequency your body requires to heal comes through your hands into your body throughout the night.

Sleep, knowing that massive repair and healing will occur as you rest.

Any time you wake up, renew your intention to deliver the frequency of healing your body requires through your hands.

A.M.

Look for pleasure.—What feels good? How is it better? Do you sense an upgrade?

Body, what are you telling me with this issue?

RENEE ROSE

Body, what do you require?

USING THE SLEEP SPA FOR EMOTIONAL OR SPIRITUAL HEALING

P.M.
Tonight I intend to be healed of:
[You might ask to heal a core wound or clear money blocks.]

_____
_____
_____
_____
_____
_____
_____

Or,
While I sleep, I will be cleared, energized, and balanced for:

_____
_____
_____
_____
_____
_____
_____

As you sleep, place your hands on your body and intend that the frequency your being requires to heal emit from your hands into your body and energetic field.

Any time you wake up or stir in the night, remind yourself of your intention for healing.

A.M.
What was healed during the night?

WRITE TO HEAL EXERCISE

*C*lose your eyes and intend to connect with your higher self / soul self. Intend it three times out loud or speaking silently:
I wish to connect to my higher self,
I wish to connect to my higher self,
I wish to connect to my higher self.

Imagine a spire at the top of your head (like a beam from a flashlight) shooting up to the ball of light above you that is your higher self. Connect in with this higher frequency. You don't have to know what I mean–just imagine it any way you like. You might imagine it's like an audio cable plugged into the jack, so you can hear what's playing up there.

_____*[Your name], what do you want to heal?* (Speak to your higher self in third person, as a separate entity. You are receiving this information as a third-party scribe. It's not your job to interpret or to participate in any way other than write down the information that comes to you.)

RENEE ROSE

Close your eyes once more and return to the image of the spire of light from the top of your head. Connect again to the ball of light that was your higher self, and now send another spire of light from that glowing sphere up to the spiritual sun that represents Source energy, or the Universe, or infinite wisdom, or God—whatever nomenclature you prefer. Repeat three times in your head or out loud:

I wish to connect to Source [or insert preferred name here] energy.
I wish to connect to Source [or insert preferred name here] energy.
I wish to connect to Source [or insert preferred name here] energy.

Source */ Universe / [Deity name of your choosing], what message do you have for* _____ *[Insert your name]?* Notice how we don't say *for me.* Again, you're the third-party scribe.

When you feel like the words have petered out and the message is complete, thank both your higher self and Source energy for the healing that took place. Affirm that you wish to disconnect with each of them three times in your head or out loud. While staying connected may seem to make more sense, it could drain or divert your energy. Consciously connecting and disconnecting is a cleaner approach and better use of your energy.

Know that your higher self heard the message from Source energy. There's nothing more you need to do. The healing has already begun and is underway. Unless you received a specific action item, you don't have to do anything more.

TOOL #5

Live to Laugh

HOME PLAY

1. Continue with your sleep spa rituals, recording and analyzing your dreams and listening to a subliminal recording while you sleep at least once a week.
2. Choose any suggestions from the following list of laughter-inducing activities that sound fun to you and follow through.

- Schedule a laughter night (or weekend, or longer!) where you watch funny movies or television shows.
- Poll your friends and compile your own list of funniest shows and movies. Figure out what you like—dumb comedies? Physical humor? The most ridiculous scenarios? Or do you prefer sarcastic or acerbic humor? Our current favorite series is *Brooklyn 99*. Other hits are *Game Changer, Tacoma FD, Parks & Rec,* and the old standby, *SNL*. Don't forget to consciously "make"

yourself laugh out loud while watching. This will feel odd at first but gets easier.
- Have a laugh party with your funniest friends
- Make your own working "joy list" and schedule it to send to yourself monthly.
- Go to a comedy club or a theater show to experience the live energy exchange of laughter. Smile and laugh out loud and be conscious of the energy exchange taking place between performer and audience.
- Attend laughter yoga, goat yoga, puppy yoga, kitten yoga, buti yoga, or any other movement form that makes you laugh out loud.
- Write a parody of your favorite song or show, even if it's just a couple of lines.
- Poll your friends and family on what is funny to them.
- Watch amusing YouTube videos or TikToks.

JOY LIST

*D*ear Future Me,
    Here are things that I enjoy:

___
___
___
___
___
___
___
___
___
___
___
___
___

Consider typing this up and schedule it to pop up as a monthly message to yourself. :-)

TOOL #6

Welcome the Wins

HOME PLAY

1. Cultivate a group of friends who will celebrate your wins.
2. Make a kick ass folder.
3. At the end of each day, record three small or large wins of the day in your *Relax to Riches* journal.
4. Catalog and celebrate every single manifestation win.
5. Plan celebrations for your future accomplishments.
6. Practice the Oneness Meditation and Sharing your Wins with a Past Self Meditation in this section.
7. Continue with your sleep spa rituals, once-a-week subliminal programming, dream analysis, and healing practices.

ONENESS MEDITATION

1. Drop your barriers (imagine the walls around you disintegrating to dust)
2. Imagine a ball of light around you, about three feet in every direction. Is your ball spherical? Or is it misshapen? Does it have dents? Is it collapsed in any area? (Don't judge, just observe.)
3. Expand your awareness out a million miles in every direction. Imagine it like a rolling expansion—it just continues on into infinity.
4. Vibe in this space of expansion. Notice the interconnectedness you feel. How you now are part of "oneness" or "all that is". In this space, you have access to everything. The answer to any questions. Any energy you desire to pull in (love, success, glory, abundance, freedom, pleasure). All you have to do is call it to you and resonate with it.
5. Remember that what you choose to vibe with is what will show up in your life. So marinating in pleasure will bring you more things that pleasure you.

6. Notice your thoughts and emotions now. Do you have a sense of infinite possibilities? Did the state of limitation disappear? How loving / grateful / joyful do you feel?
7. Note that this is YOU. You are this infinite space. This infinite wisdom. This beautiful being of light. You aren't your limiting beliefs or the personal construct you often function from. You are so much more. You are a goddess. A being of magnitude.
8. Repeat often and throughout the day. Anytime you feel "less-than". Anytime your thoughts bog you down. Any time you want more. This is the space of receiving.

MEDITATION TO SHARE YOUR WINS WITH YOUR PAST SELF

1. Drop your barriers (imagine the walls or armor around you disintegrating).
2. Expand your awareness out a million miles in every direction. Imagine it like a rolling expansion—it just continues on into infinity.
3. Call in your higher self. See it as a ball of light that descends from above and surrounds you.
4. Now invite in any part or piece of you who may be in resistance or is triggered by something. If you don't have one in mind, just see what shows up.
5. Where in your body do you feel it?
6. How old is that part? In other words, what age were you when that part came into existence? Is she from this lifetime or another?
7. If there is a particular memory associated with the creation of the part or piece of you, ask her to show you what she experienced or what she believes.
8. Thank this part for showing you the memory or sharing with you their beliefs. Thank them for trying to keep you

safe and protected. For trying to warn you against danger.

9. Show this part all you have achieved. Show this part what year it is. That you're all grown up. That you are a successful, wonderful person who has achieved many things. Show them a few of the accomplishments you are most proud of.
10. Let them see that their fears are unfounded. If this was a piece from your childhood, show them that you're all grown up now. You have agency and can't be scooped up or mishandled or abused in any way. Show them some of your successes. If it's from a past life, show the reality you live in here and now.
11. Now, ask if they'd be willing to take a step back and let you lead. Or if they could find another way supporting you. Tell them you don't even have to know what that way is.
12. When you feel like you have their agreement, ask if there are any other parts within you who wish to speak or who are afraid something dangerous might happen with the updates you just made. If there are, go through the same process with those parts.
13. When you're finished, thank all your parts. Notice that expansion comes with having your higher self leading and guiding. That sense of unconditional love, of gratitude, of abundance. Can you sense how relevant and important it was to make sure that all of you is on board with welcoming your wins? How much more empowered and whole you feel when all of you can really receive where you are now and what you're capable of?

GENERATIVE QUESTIONS

Where am I most productive?

RENEE ROSE

. . .

What is hot about me?

RENEE ROSE

Why do people love my work?

What else is possible in this situation now?

RENEE ROSE

Where are my days filled with inspiration?

Why do I make friends everywhere I go?

RENEE ROSE

Why do so many people love and support me?

How did I get so good at making and receiving money?

TOOL #7

Consume Cannibals

HOME PLAY

1. Continue with your sleep spa ritual.
2. At least once a week, listen to a subliminal recording as you sleep.
3. Record, analyze, and heal any dream content that comes up.
4. Play with any meditation in this section that speaks to you.

EXERCISE TO EXPAND OUT

1. Drop your barriers (imagine the walls around you disintegrating to dust).
2. Imagine a ball of light around you, about three feet in every direction. Is your ball spherical? Or is it misshapen? Does it have dents? Is it collapsed in any area? (Don't judge, just observe.)
3. Expand your awareness out a million miles in every direction. Imagine it like a rolling expansion—it just continues on into infinity.
4. Vibe in this space of expansion. Notice the interconnectedness you feel. How you now are part of "oneness" or "all that is". In this space, you have access to everything. You have the answer to any questions. Any energy you desire to pull in (love, success, glory, abundance, freedom, pleasure). All you have to do is call it to you and resonate with it.
5. Remember that what you choose to vibe with is what will show up in your life. Marinating in pleasure will bring you more things that pleasure you.

6. Notice your thoughts and emotions now. Do you have a sense of infinite possibilities? Did the state of limitation disappear? How loving / grateful / joyful do you feel?
7. Note that this is YOU. You are this infinite space. This infinite wisdom. This beautiful being of light. You aren't your limiting beliefs or the personal construct you often function from. You are so much more. You are a vibrational being. A being of magnitude.
8. Repeat often and throughout the day. Anytime you feel "less-than". Anytime your thoughts bog you down. Any time you want more. This is the space of receiving.
9. Imagine a ball of light around you, about three feet in every direction. Is your ball spherical? Or is it misshapen? Does it have dents? Is it collapsed in any area? (Don't judge, just observe.)
10. Expand your awareness out a million miles in every direction. Imagine it like a rolling expansion–it just continues on into infinity.
11. Vibe in this space of expansion. Notice the interconnectedness you feel. How you now are part of "oneness" or "all that is". In this space, you have access to everything. You have the answer to any questions. Any energy you desire to pull in (love, success, glory, abundance, freedom, pleasure). All you have to do is call it to you and resonate with it.
12. Remember that what you choose to vibe with is what will show up in your life. Marinating in pleasure will bring you more things that pleasure you.
13. Notice your thoughts and emotions now. Do you have a sense of infinite possibilities? Did the state of limitation disappear? How loving / grateful / joyful do you feel?
14. Note that this is YOU. You are this infinite space. This infinite wisdom. This beautiful being of light. You aren't your limiting beliefs or the personal construct you often function from. You are so much more. You are a vibrational being. A being of magnitude.

15. Repeat often and throughout the day. Anytime you feel "less-than". Anytime your thoughts bog you down. Any time you want more. This is the space of receiving.

CONSUME CANNIBALS MEDITATION

1. Drop your barriers and expand out a million miles in every direction. [It's useful to expand before you start playing with energy when working with others, so their energy is diluted and won't affect you.]
2. Imagine the other person and all their fronting and boasting as a ball of light.
3. Put a straw into the ball of light and suck, sipping from their projection onto you.
4. Rather than listening to or feeling what particular energies are embodied in their field, because below all that bluster is likely a deep sense of unworthiness, you are simply receiving. This exercise isn't about receiving the particular energy that they have or don't have. It's about putting you in a state of receiving around someone who is peacocking. The energy flow changes from one of them pushing energy at you to one of you genuinely receiving from them. They will likely relax their "fronting," and you will share a more genuine human connection, a state of listening and receiving. The state of communion between two souls.

MEDITATION TO FLOW ENERGY WITH ANOTHER

1. Drop your barriers (imagine the walls around you disintegrating to dust).
2. Imagine a ball of light around you, about three feet in every direction. Is your ball spherical? Or is it freeform? Does it have dents? Is it collapsed in any area? (Don't judge, just observe.)
3. Expand your ball of light and awareness out a million miles in every direction. Imagine it like a rolling expansion—it just continues on into infinity.
4. Call to mind the person you wish to play with. Picture them with a ball of light around them as well.
5. With giant, invisible "scoopy hands," pull all the energy of the Universe in through the back of the heart-center (between their shoulder blades) of the person you're working with.
6. That energy flows through them and out the front of their heart-center into the center of your heart.
7. It flows out the back of your heart and a small spire of it returns to the person, so they get some of your energy back.

8. You can choose to draw through them a particular energy, like "love" or "gratitude". I was feeling unappreciated at work many years ago, and I drew "respect" through my boss, and it changed our relationship.
9. Now, reverse the flow. Pull all the energy of the Universe with giant invisible scoopy hands through the back of your heart-center, out the front of your heart, into the front of their heart, and out their back, with a small spire returning to you.
10. You can just send energy in general or pick a particular frequency you'd like to share.
11. You may find they are blocked to receiving from you. In this case, try pulling through them and receiving from them, then try again. You could also try turning down the flow to a small trickle or intend that it flow on the waveform that's acceptable to them and they can receive.
12. Play with the sending and receiving until the flow feels easy and flowing in both directions.

HOT AIR BALLOON MEDITATION

1. Close your eyes, drop your barriers, and expand a million miles out and every direction.
2. Call to mind the person or people you wish to release from your energetic field.
3. Imagine their joyful departure. You are standing on the ground ready to bid them farewell. They climb in the basket. You might take their photos. As the basket of the beautiful hot air balloon lifts off into the sunrise or sunset, they smile and wave at you. They lift off higher and higher, joyful at their new adventure that is separate and away from you. Congratulate them on their choice to align with what's in their highest good.
4. Send them your thanks for the role they played in your life or just experience gratitude that they are gone. Either way, gratitude is an energy that expands.
5. Know that you have changed the energy between the two of you. The change might not be as fast as the fifteen minutes it took for the dancer to quit after I did this meditation, but things will shift. Trust that.
6. Notice what's different the next time you interact with this person.
7. Repeat the meditation anytime you fall into doubt or get frustrated about this person.

CORD CLEARING MEDITATION

1. Call your highest self and picture it like a ball of light that descends from above and surrounds you.
2. Picture the other person in front of you. Call in their highest self and imagine their light ball descending from above and surrounding them.
3. Ask that any energetic cords that extend from you to them unhook and return. I like to picture the cords like fishing lines. I pull the hooks out of the other person and reel my cord back to me.
4. Plug the loose end into your heart, so you're seeking energy only from yourself, not others.
5. Unhook or unplug any hooks or cords that are plugged into you from them and send them back to them. Plug their ends back into their heart, so they may be responsible for their own energy and can dwell in their own energetic field.
6. Say out loud or in your head, *Any responsibility I gave you for my life, I now take back.* Notice if you have any resistance to saying that and observe what, if anything, comes back.

7. Say out loud or in your head, *I return to you all responsibility for your life that I have taken.* Notice the energy as it returns to them. If you get a hit on what areas you have taken responsibility for their life, note it in your *Relax to Riches* journal and affirm that you are no longer taking responsibility there.
8. Say out loud or in your head, *I forgive you. I release all unforgiveness.* Notice how the second statement feels different from the first. I always find a little something more releases when I add the second part.
9. Say out loud or in your head, *I am free, and you are free.*
10. You might close with the Hawaiian Ho'oponopono Healing prayer, which is another great way to release energetic enmeshment. Say or think the words *I love You, I'm Sorry, Forgive Me, Thank You* in any order that feels good to you.

TOOL #8

Purge Pain

HOME PLAY

1. Continue with your sleep spa ritual.
2. At least once a week, listen to a subliminal recording as you sleep.
3. Record, analyze, and heal any dream content that comes up.
4. Try out a mind-body somatic practice this week, like EFT, yoga, Feldenkrais(R) Method, energy work, tuning forks, or sound healing.
5. Practice the meditation Releasing Trauma at a Cellular Level included in this section.
6. Complete the freewriting exercise and meditation to heal a resistant part of you.

RELEASING TRAUMA AT A CELLULAR LEVEL

Here **is a simple process for releasing trauma from your cells:**

1. Close your eyes, drop your barriers, and expand your energy out a million miles in every direction.
2. Imagine the bright white light of the spiritual sun descending from above and surrounding your head, moving downward through your entire body and out your feet and into the center core of Earth.
3. Imagine a bright green that represents the light of nature / Gaia / Earth energy rising through the soles of your feet and up your legs, bathing your knees, your hips, your belly, your heart, your throat, and finally your head, then traveling all the way up to the spiritual sun.
4. Ask for cellular memory of any pain or trauma (or a specific one) to dissipate and release through all levels, layers, timelines, and dimensions.
5. Imagine it releasing from you like a cloud of smoke or fog that emits from your form.

6. Watch as it dissipates and releases back to the Earth, back to the ether, to be transmitted and absorbed by all-that-is.
7. Notice if there is a scent associated with your new, cleansed self.
8. Is there a wild animal or mythical creature you associate with your new, cleansed self? Choose one for yourself now.
9. Know that you made space for new possibilities and your energetic body. Recalling your animal and the scent whenever the trauma bubbles up will provide an anchor for your subconscious to return to this lightened state and help it to become permanent.

UNCOVER A RESISTANT PART

*F*reewrite on the following prompt –
What part of me is in resistance to _____ [the thing I am trying to manifest]?

_____
_____
_____
_____
_____
_____
_____
_____
_____
_____
_____
_____
_____
_____

What is this part of me afraid of?

What age is this part of me?

What other places in my life do I feel this way?

When was the first time I felt this way? What happened then?

With the knowledge gained from your freewriting, try a meditation where you speak to that part to help her heal. If you prefer to do it with a therapist, please do so.

If you feel comfortable, try the following meditation to meet with a traumatized / pained part of yourself. I highly recommend working with a professional if you require support in this process.

WORKING WITH A PART OF YOURSELF (VARIATION)

1. Sit or lie down with your eyes closed and imagine you're standing on the top of a beautiful crystal mountain. Ask if there's a part of yourself that experienced trauma that would like to communicate with you.
2. Where do you feel they reside in your body? For example, do you feel a tightness in your chest when you think about them?
3. Invite them to meet you on the top of this crystal mountain.
4. Face them with total allowance, compassion, and approval. They are not an adversary to try to clear or work against. They are showing up to help you, to share knowledge with you, to help you integrate.
5. Ask what they want to tell you about what happened to them.
6. Ask what gift they're trying to give you. Are they trying to keep you safe or protect you in some way? To keep you in a state of high alert or warning against danger?
7. Listen with total approval. No judgment. Massive compassion.
8. Thank them for those gifts.
9. If the gift is unwanted, tell them you no longer require this form of protection. You appreciate their help, but you can take it from here.

10. Ask them if they can find a new way to stand at your side or behind you and support you.
11. Thank them again for coming and sharing this buried part of you. Allow the scene to dissolve and return to the present.
12. Notice if the initial feeling in your body has changed.

TOOL #9

Give Up Guilt

HOME PLAY

1. Continue with your sleep spa ritual.
2. At least once a week, listen to a subliminal recording as you sleep.
3. Record, analyze, and heal any dream content that comes up.
4. Freewrite on the prompts that follow this page.
5. Do the Cord Clearing Meditation or the Space Clearing Meditation.

IDENTIFYING GUILT OR SHAME

The places I am controlled by shame the most are....

_____
_____
_____
_____
_____
_____
_____
_____
_____
_____
_____
_____
_____

… RELAX TO RICHES WORKBOOK

RENEE ROSE

I still have shame about…

My secret fear is that I'm a bad person because…

MEDITATION TO CLEAR SPACE

Try this meditation with me to clear space and change everyone you're relating to into a circle of you.

1. Get comfortable—sit or lie down. Close your eyes and drop your barriers.
2. Expand your awareness and the bubble of light you perceive around you out a million miles in every direction.
3. Continue to imagine that expansion going into infinity.
4. Send a spire of energy (like the beam of a flashlight) down through the soles of your feet into the center core of the Earth, connecting into the grid of light of the Earth.
5. Imagine a spire coming out the top of your head, connecting into the spiritual sun above you.
6. Picture a giant snow plow and use it to plow energetic space all around you in every direction until you have a large area of space that only contains your energy.
7. Around the perimeter of the circle you plowed, imagine

replicas of you all standing shoulder to shoulder in a circle facing you.
8. This is the group you will now be relating to. This is the group whose opinion you will ask.
9. When you're worried about how others may judge you, it is only this group of others you will see or seek. Does this group judge you? What do they think is best for you? What do they want from you?
10. Anytime throughout your day that you feel that pinch or contraction from thinking a thought that brings you shame or from feeling shameful or not enough, return to this image. You have space around you, and you're surrounded by the circle of you. What do you think / feel / know about the situation?

ADDITIONAL PAGES

RELAX TO RICHES WORKBOOK

RENEE ROSE

RENEE ROSE

RENEE ROSE

RENEE ROSE

RENEE ROSE

RENEE ROSE

RENEE ROSE

RENEE ROSE

…

RENEE ROSE

RENEE ROSE

RENEE ROSE

RENEE ROSE

RENEE ROSE

RENEE ROSE

RELAX TO RICHES WORKBOOK

ABOUT RENEE ROSE

15-time *USA Today* **bestselling romance author Renee Rose** is passionate about helping other authors find and maintain an abundance mindset to catapult their careers and create their best future. She employs energetic tools and techniques to help her clients clear resistance and money blocks, access their inner guidance, and tap into their love and appreciation for their books so they can achieve their dreams.

www.write2riches.com
renee@reneeroseromance.com

facebook.com/writetoriches
instagram.com/writetoriches
amazon.com/Renee-Rose/e/B008AS0FT0
bookbub.com/authors/renee-rose
tiktok.com/@write2riches

www.ingramcontent.com/pod-product-compliance
Lightning Source LLC
Chambersburg PA
CBHW060605080526
44585CB00013B/684